Happy Together

Hollywood's
Unforgettable Couples

Edited by
Peter W. Engelmeier

Texts written by
Sabine Behrends

Prestel

Munich · Berlin · London · New York

The Actors and Actresses

The Films

The two halves of a couple — taken together — make up more than a whole… God knows why, but that's how it is! Woody Allen

Peter W. Engelmeier

What would Tarzan be without Jane or Laurel without Hardy?

Relaxing with a picture book isn't really something you can share with anyone else. Most people prefer to flick through the pages on their own, lost in daydreams conjured up by the images.

Do you prefer to be left alone or do you enjoy someone else's company? Do you want to shut out the real world or do you like to share the limelight with the couples in *Happy Together*?

Film books, that remind us of what we have seen and enjoyed in the past, tend to give rise to nostalgic feelings, making us exclaim "Do you remember that scene . . .?" and "Wasn't that great . . .!" There's no doubt that it's consoling to be able to wing yourself back to the darkness of the cinema; it's exciting to recall scenes and images from the screen, to share these with someone special, and to consider the effect movies have on the way we see things.

Happy Together is about screen couples and the fascination they hold for us. It goes in search of the felicitous force that two actors — seemingly happy together — can produce. It can be so strong as to become an end in itself; their 'game of doubles' can be a source of more stimulus and excitement for viewers than the feats of a lone hero (regardless of how compelling or amusing). It's a matter of taste whether one would rather watch the lonesome cowboy or the antics of Laurel and Hardy. There's no doubt in my mind: two virtuoso actors in a masterly face-to-face duo are by far preferable to a solo virtuoso delving the depths of his own ego with no one to look in the eye (apart from the viewer, that is). Just picture Tarzan without Jane, and you'll know what I mean.

What memorable couples are there? Comedy duos, like Jerry Lewis and Dean Martin, playing off each other with gags that cause even more sparks to fly and with scripts that make the most of their eccentric gestures and facial expressions; dancing couples, like Ginger Rogers and Fred Astaire, spinning around and ready to support the other if need be; society stars like Greta Garbo and Melvyn Douglas, for whom composure is a basic instinct; tragic criminals like Bonnie and Clyde (Faye Dunaway and Warren Beatty), whose criminal energies arise mainly from their need to impress each other, and whose murderous activities take them beyond their ordinary lives—just like Thelma and Louise (Susan Sarandon and Geena Davis). There are the love story tragedians like Ali MacGraw and Ryan O'Neal, whose tears are synonymous with undying love beyond the grave; and there are the odd couples like Harold and Maude (Ruth Gordon and Bud Cort), whose peculiarities are compounded when we see them alongside each other in their own bizarre worlds. Other couples' marital bliss turns into mutual loathing and violence, as demonstrated by the Roses in their domestic war (Kathleen Turner and Michel Douglas), which sees the last of the Ming heirlooms being smashed to pieces on the floor. And finally there are the lovers of a class like Marilyn Monroe and Laurence Olivier (*The Prince and the Showgirl*). They have come to be inseparable screen icons who trigger signals in the minds of fans that in turn give rise to images ranging from the sensual to the lascivious. Indeed, they are sometimes so erotic that couples in real life base their own love life on that of cinema's immortal lovers. Kim Basinger and Mickey Rourke in *Nine ½ Weeks* were *the* role models for many a progressive couple in the 1990s. Or take the fairy-tale figures of Julia Roberts and Richard Gere in *Pretty Woman*, the film that showed how even millionaires have no problems in rehabilitating streetwalkers if they happen to look attractive.

I sigh on thinking about the couples who were just that: couples on the screen and in real life, the Katharine Hepburns and Spencer Tracys of this world who played themselves when they cast as successful partners (and whose private life had something of the cinema about it).

What more could one want when flicking through the albums of film history? Apart from someone to share the experience with, that is.

"Kiss Me, Kate…"

Doug and Mary, Hollywood's first great dream couple, playing Shakespeare

The Taming of the Shrew 1929

DIRECTOR Sam Taylor; written by: Sam Taylor, based on the play of the same name by William Shakespeare; cinematographer: Karl Struss; editing: Allen McNeil

WITH Mary Pickford (Katharine), Douglas Fairbanks (Petruchio), Edwin Maxwell (Baptista), Joseph Cawthorn (Gremio), Clyde Cook (Grumio), Geoffrey Wardwell (Hortensio), Dorothy Jordan (Bianca), Charles Stevens (servant)

Douglas Fairbanks and
Mary Pickford, 1917

The film world's first dream couple was Douglas Fairbanks Sr. and Mary Pickford, the "King and Queen of Hollywood," as they were called. They were exceptional people in every respect. He was a handsome man with a winning smile and an athletic physique who performed almost all his own stunts. An idol surrounded by admirers, he set women's pulses racing and had box-office tills ringing. She was young, pretty and moved people with her beauty, was *the* star of the silent screen and was hailed as "America's Sweetheart." Both of them first trod the boards as youngsters. Douglas Fairbanks made his Broadway debut in 1902 and moved to Hollywood in 1915 after studying at Harvard and traveling through Europe. He played his last role in 1934 and then went into retirement. Mary Pickford was sixteen when she made her first film and retired aged forty-three—having made 236 films!

Douglas Fairbanks and Mary Pickford were not only highly successful as actors, but as scriptwriters and producers, too. In 1919, along with Charlie Chaplin and D.W. Griffith, they founded the United Artists Corporation that went on to produce outstanding films over the next sixty years before its takeover by MGM. The two of them were also among the thirty-six co-founders of the Academy of Motion Picture Arts and Sciences, the body that awards the Oscars annually. Douglas Fairbanks was its first president and Mary Pickford was the second actress to receive an Oscar as best leading lady.

These prolific actors, who were husband and wife for sixteen years, made only one film together, *The Taming of the Shrew*. Half of Shakespeare's text sufficed for them to tell the well-known tale of Katharine and her husband Petruchio. An entertaining film with decent box-office takings, it was, however, not nearly as successful as the films in which they appeared individually.

"I... ain't... so tough..."

Tough on the outside, soft inside: Tom Powers' dying words

The Public Enemy 1931

DIRECTOR William A. Wellman; written by: Harvey Thew, based on the story "Beer and Blood" by Kubec Glasmon and John Bright; cinematographer: Dev Jennings; music: David Mendoza; editing: Ed McCormick

WITH Jean Harlow (Gwen Allen), James Cagney (Tom Powers), Edward Woods (Matt Doyle), Joan Blondell (Mamie), Beryl Mercer (Ma Powers), Donald Cook (Mike Powers), Mae Clarke (Kitty), Leslie Fenton (Nails Nathan), Murray Kinnell (Putty Nose)

This was the first major success for James Cagney, already aged thirty-two, and it established his stardom. It was not until 1930 that he first stood in front of a film camera, and in the role of Tom Powers he came to symbolize the petty criminal on his way up, a man who from his early years has learned how organized crime works and who is now a master of it. He played the part so convincingly that in the years to come he was hired time and again for similar roles. The gangster image was one he was never able to shake off.

Cagney was paired with a platinum blonde, Jean Harlow, who had also garnered her first major film honors only the year before. Harlow was an eccentric figure among the circle of Hollywood actors. Even as young as twenty-three, she had been divorced twice and widowed once. Her second husband shot himself after eight weeks of married life. She died aged twenty-six, probably due to kidney failure, but would have been saved had her mother, a member of a strict sect, not refused her medical help.

The genre of the gangster film became established with *The Public Enemy*. Never before had the brutality of criminals been so vividly shown on screen. The realistic depiction of violence set the style for a whole genre whose heyday still lay in the future.

"You are a crook. I want you as a crook. I love you as a crook."

Lily Vautier reminding Gaston what he's supposed to be doing

Trouble in Paradise   1932

DIRECTOR Ernst Lubitsch; written by: Grover Jones, Samson Raphaelson, based on the comedy *The Honest Finder* by Laszlo Aladar; cinematographer: Victor Milner; music: W. Franke Harling

WITH Miriam Hopkins (Lily Vautier), Herbert Marshall (Gaston Monescu alias La Valle), Kay Francis (Mariette Colet), Charlie Ruggles (Major), Edward Everett Horton (François Filiba), C. Aubrey Smith (Adolph Giron), Robert Greig (Jacques the butler), George Humbert (waiter)

Herbert Marshall with Kay Francis (left) and Miriam Hopkins (right)

Ernst Lubitsch was a precocious film-maker, producing his first silent film in Berlin in 1913 aged twenty-one. He would become one of the best comedy directors that Hollywood studios had ever had. There was something special about his films; the 'Lubitsch touch' was characterized by a graceful, light and restrained style, witty dialogues and the urbanity of the big, wide world and those who inhabit it. *Trouble in Paradise* tells the story of an attractive pair of small-time crooks, Lily (Miriam Hopkins) and Gaston Monescu (Herbert Marshall), who mistakenly believe each other to be wealthy and worth stealing from. Having rifled through each other's pockets during a dinner, they decide to work together in future and to look out for more rewarding targets. Their next victim turns up in the shape of Madame Colet (Kay Francis), the rich widow of a perfume manufacturer. She quickly sees through the two of them, but goes along with the charming Gaston's ruse. In the end, he looses the desire to rob her and instead wants to stay put in "paradise." When their cover is about to be blown, he has no choice but to go ahead with the robbery and do a runner with Lily.

Shortly afterwards, Lubitsch filmed *Design for Living* with Miriam Hopkins whose work he greatly admired. She had been unknown up until that point, but these two films put her on the road to success in Hollywood. Kay Francis was already a star at Warner Brothers. Lubitsch next worked with Herbert Marshall on a film called *Angel* for whose female lead Marlene Dietrich was hired.

"Me Tarzan, You Jane."

Communication, jungle-style

Tarzan the Ape Man 1932

DIRECTOR Woodbridge Strong Van Dyke; written by: Cyril Hume, Ivor Novello, based on the story by Edgar Rice Burroughs; cinematography: Harold Rosson, Clyde De Vinna; editing: Ben Lewis, Tom Held

WITH Maureen O'Sullivan (Jane Parker), Johnny Weissmuller (Tarzan), Neil Hamilton (Harry Holt), C. Aubrey Smith (James Parker), Doris Lloyd (Mrs. Cutten), Forrester Harvey (Beamish), Ivory Williams (Riano)

Raised by a female ape, Tarzan, the white lord of the animals, became a legendary Hollywood figure, and the men who played him all became stars. The most famous of them was Johnny Weissmuller, who played the role eleven times. On six occasions, his leading lady was Maureen O'Sullivan, the mother Mia Farrow's.

The first film to star Johnny Weissmuller tells the story of two adventurers, James Parker and Harry Holt, who are in Africa to search for elephants' graveyards and ivory. Parker's pretty daughter Jane joins them unexpectedly. When Tarzan catches a glimpse of her, he whisks her straight off to his tree house, but he soon frees her again and she returns to the expedition. When the group is attacked a short while later, a desperate Jane sends the ape Cheetah to Tarzan for help. After he rescues them, Jane decides to stay with him. His few words—"Me Tarzan, you Jane"—suffice to make a happy couple of them.

The film is driven by shots of the jungle and the unusual stunts that Johnny Weissmuller performed himself. Clad in a narrow loincloth, he swung through the jungle from liana to liana, uttering a blood-curdling cry that not only had herds of elephants tramping to his aid but also had fans pouring into cinemas to see him.

"Can I offer you anything? Frosted chocolate? Cointreau? Benedictine? Marriage?"

Guy Holden's offers to Mimi Glossop

The Gay Divorcee   1934

DIRECTOR Mark Sandrich; written by: George Marion Jr., Dorothy Yost, Edward Kaufman, based on the musical of the same name by Cole Porter and Dwight Taylor; cinematographer: David Abel; music: Max Steiner; editing: William Hamilton

WITH Ginger Rogers (Mimi Glossop), Fred Astaire (Guy Holden), Alice Brady (Hortense Ditherwell), Edward Everett Horton (Egbert Fitzgerald), Erik Rhodes (Rodolfo Tonetti), Eric Blore (waiter), Lillian Miles (hotel guest), Charles Coleman (valet), William Austin (Cyril Glossop)

Ginger Rogers and Fred Astaire were the very personification of the Hollywood dancing team. Over a period of sixteen years, the two of them were to star in ten films together. *The Gay Divorcee* was their second film, and it was immediately nominated for the Oscar for Best Film.

In 1932, the original show had had a Broadway run of seven months and received mediocre reviews. The music of Cole Porter, however, was well received, especially the song "Night and Day."

After Ginger Rogers and Fred Astaire had made a huge impression in their first joint film (they appeared only in minor roles), RKO immediately gave them the opportunity to work together again. This is a comedy of mistaken identities in which Ginger Rogers erroneously thinks Astaire, in the guise of her supposed lover, is the man who will help her get a divorce. The film is driven by many wonderful dance sequences. Astaire was already known for self-discipline: he would rehearse every step and movement until they were just perfect and until they could be executed with a lightness that betrayed nothing of the sheer hard work that underlay them. The climax of all his dancing scenes is the one where his steps seduce Ginger Rogers to the strains of Cole Porter's "Night and Day" and where she finally falls in love with him.

Federico Fellini later paid special homage to Astaire and Rogers in a film about an elderly pair of dancers (played by Marcello Mastroianni and Giulietta Masina) who in their early years had emulated Ginger and Fred, Hollywood's legendary dancing partners.

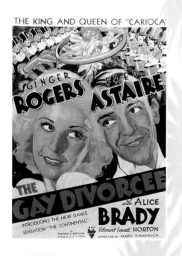

> # *"Your right eye says yes, and your left eye says no. Fifi, you're cockeyed!"*

Danilo to Sonia

The Merry Widow 1934

DIRECTOR Ernst Lubitsch; written by: Samson Raphaelson, Ernest Vajda, based on the operetta of the same name by Franz Lehár; cinematographer: Oliver T. Marsh; music: Herbert Stothart; editing: Frances Marsh

WITH Jeanette MacDonald (Sonia), Maurice Chevalier (Prince Danilo), Edward Everett Horton (Ambassador Popoff), Una Merkel (Queen Dolores), George Barbier (King Achmed), Minna Gombell (Marcelle), Ruth Channing (Lulu), Sterling Holloway (Mischka)

The Merry Widow was based on Franz Lehár's renowned operetta and was Ernst Lubitsch's last musical before he devoted himself completely to screwball comedy. Lubitsch was a master of amusing and intelligent entertainment films, and here again he cast Maurice Chevalier and sassy Jeanette MacDonald in the leading roles. She was an actress with an outstanding voice and great Broadway successes under her belt and she rose to new honors with the growing popularity of the Hollywood musical. Chevalier, originally a Parisian café singer, arrived in Hollywood in 1929. His first role was a flop, but his second one, *The Love Parade*, with Jeanette MacDonald and directed by Ernst Lubitsch that same year, was a success. Chevalier and MacDonald co-starred in another musical, *Love me Tonight*, in 1932, directed for Paramount by Rouben Mamoulian.

Maurice Chevalier remained true to the genre of the musical throughout his career. One of his best roles was that of an old actor partnering Leslie Caron in *Gigi*. His rendition of the song "Thank God for little Girls" is among the film's best scenes.

"...like a Dior creation"

Charlie Chaplin describing Paulette Goddard's costumes in *Modern Times*,
which demanded a great deal of thought and finesse

Modern Times 1936

DIRECTOR, WRITER AND MUSIC
Charles Chaplin; cinematography:
Roland H. Totheroh, Ira Morgan

WITH Charles Chaplin (Charlie), Paulette
Goddard (Gamine), Henry Bergman (café
owner), Allan Garcia (factory owner),
Chester Conklin (mechanic), Stanley J.
Sanford (Big Bill, worker), Stanley Blystone
(Sheriff Couler), Sam Stein (foreman)

Paulette Goddard and
Charles Chaplin in private

Modern Times was the fifth of the evening-long feature films that Charlie
Chaplin produced for United Artists starting in 1923 and it would also
be his last silent film. He always needed a lengthy period of preparation
before he was able to start shooting. The film was inspired by a conver-
sation Chaplin had with a journalist who described to him the assembly
line production methods in Detroit's factories and the effects they had
on workers. The most famous scene is the one where Charlie, strug-
gling to cope with the speed of the assembly line, is finally defeated by it
and is drawn into the machine. Like the materials being manufactured,
he winds his way between cogs and wheels, finally emerging from the
production line dazed and battered like after a bad dream. He is
arrested, but while being whisked away in a Black Maria meets a blind
flower seller who ensures a happy, if somewhat delicate end.

The woman at his side was a young Paulette Goddard whom Chaplin met on a friend's yacht. She was recently divorced and new in Hollywood; he was very lonely, as he later admitted, and they both spent a
great deal of time in each other's company. When they finished shooting *Modern Times*, they set sail for Hong Kong. In the course of the
months-long crossing, they married. They collaborated again on *The
Great Dictator* before they went their separate ways after eight years' of
marriage.

Stan: "You remember how dumb I used to be?"

Stan has the feeling that he's better now

Block-Heads 1938

DIRECTOR John B. Blystone; written by: Charles Rogers, Felix Adler, James Parrott, Harry Langdon, Arnold Belgard; cinematographer: Art Lloyd; editing: Bert Jordan

WITH Stan Laurel (Mr. Laurel), Oliver Hardy (Mr. Hardy), Minna Gombell (Mrs. Hardy), Billy Gilbert (Mr. Gilbert), Patricia Ellis (Mrs. Gilbert), James Finlayson (Mr. Finn)

Stan Laurel (right, in both photos) and Oliver Hardy as block-heads

Generations of movie-goers have laughed at the gags of Laurel and Hardy, a comedy team that in every respect was a class of its own. The list of all the films, long and short, in which Oliver Hardy appeared numbers over 400; Stan Laurel chalked up almost 200. They did not only work as actors but also wrote scripts and directed while Stan Laurel even produced films. They first appeared together in a film in 1919. Ten years later, they were full-time collaborators turning out one short after another, and in the 1930s, they began to make feature films. In *Block-Heads*, Stan is unaware that World War I has been over for twenty years and still goes about in his uniform. His friend Ollie removes him from the Veterans' Home and takes him to his house so that his wife can cook Stan's meals. She, however, has other plans and disappears. One gag follows another in the course of the film's ninety minutes. Ollie thinks Stan has had a leg amputated (in fact, he has tucked a leg underneath him while sitting in his wheelchair) and out of sympathy Ollie carries Stan around all the time until he notices that his friend does indeed have two legs. The audience is witness to their attempts at cooking and the ruination of Ollie's wife's kitchen. And there's more....

As successful as Laurel and Hardy's films still were in the 1930s, their popularity dwindled during World War II. They made their last film together in 1952—the last we heard and saw of this great comedy duo.

"Don't flatter yourself.
I'm not a marrying man."

Straight talk from Rhett Butler

Gone with the Wind

1939

DIRECTOR Victor Fleming; written by: Sidney Howard, based on the novel of the same name by Margaret Mitchell; cinematography: Ernest Haller, Ray Rennahan; music: Max Steiner; editing: Hal C. Kern, James E. Newcom

WITH Vivien Leigh (Scarlett O'Hara), Clark Gable (Rhett Butler), Olivia de Haviland (Melanie Hamilton), Leslie Howard (Ashley Wilkes), Thomas Mitchell (Gerald O'Hara), Hattie McDaniel (Mammy)

Gone with the Wind is one of the great screen classics and in 1977 was nominated best film of all time by the American Film Institute. It was based on the one novel that journalist Margaret Mitchell was to write in her life. MGM would not be hurried in its search for the right cast for this blockbuster film, and even if Clark Gable was swiftly cast in the role of Rhett Butler, the search for the true Scarlett O'Hara was a long one. Every famous Hollywood actress of the day coveted the role, but in the end, the successful actress was Englishwoman Vivien Leigh, whom no one in the United States had heard of until then. This pairing proved to be a huge stroke of luck: rarely have two stars succeeded in becoming so completely engrossed in their roles. Nonetheless, Clark Gable was unable to read the whole novel by way of preparation for his role and, beaten by it, he gave up halfway through. Reading just wasn't one of his strengths....

It took three directors—Victor Fleming was the one who, in the end, was mentioned in the credits—to develop the tragic love affair, set against the backdrop of the American Civil War, between two social outcasts unable to live together despite what they have in common. Almost four hours long, this epic motion picture swept the board at the next awards ceremony, winning a total of ten Oscars.

"I'm so happy! I'm so happy! Nobody can be so happy without being punished."

Ninotchka to Leon

Ninotchka 1939

DIRECTOR Ernst Lubitsch; written by: Charles Brackett, Billy Wilder and Walter Reisch, based on an idea by Melchior Lengyel; cinematographer: William Daniels; music: Werner R. Heymann; editing: Gene Ruggiero

WITH Greta Garbo (Ninotchka), Melvyn Douglas (Count Léon d'Algout), Sig Rumann (Iranoff), Alexander Granach (Kopalski), Felix Bressart (Buljanoff), Bela Lugosi (Detective Superintendent Razinin), Ina Claire (Countess Swana)

"Garbo laughs!" ran the slogan that was used to promote the only comedy that the "divine" Garbo was to make in her career. MGM hired Ernst Lubitsch to direct it, a man highly regarded by Garbo, who in this film plays an austere and glowering Soviet commissar ordered to Paris where three comrades appear to have forgotten their mission thanks to the life of luxury they are living. It falls to Ninotchka to re-direct them on to the path of Soviet virtue, but she, too, lets herself be seduced, not least by the charms of a Melvyn Douglas in the role of the sophisticated Count Léon d'Algout. She has to leave, however, and she and her three comrades find themselves back in their workaday Soviet lives of shared rooms and food rations. But where love blossoms, it finds a way to its fulfilment. Before she has had much time to read the Count's heavily censored letters and to reflect on her visit to Paris, Ninotchka is called to Constantinople where again she has to try to make her three insubordinate comrades see reason. The Count, however, is behind it all, and so a happy ending is assured and the three comrades open a Russian restaurant in town.

The film is driven by its polished dialogue that was written by Billy Wilder with others. And the scene where Greta Garbo laughs at a clumsy Melvyn Douglas has gone down in cinematic history. For her portrayal of Ninotchka, Greta Garbo received her fourth Oscar nomination, but on this occasion the prize went to another actress, Vivien Leigh, for her performance as Scarlett O'Hara.

"Oh, we're going to talk about me again, are we? Goody!"

Tracy Lord always at the center of the action

The Philadelphia Story 1940

DIRECTOR George Cukor; written by: Donald Ogden Stewart, Waldo Salt, based on a play by Philip Barry; cinematographer: Joseph Ruttenberg; music: Franz Waxman; editing: Frank Sullivan

WITH Katharine Hepburn (Tracy Lord), Cary Grant (C.K. Dexter Haven), James Stewart (Macauley Connor), Ruth Hussey (Elizabeth Imbrie), John Howard (George Kittredge), Roland Young (Uncle Willie), John Halliday (Seth Lord), Mary Nash (Margaret Lord)

Viewed as bad news at the box office in the 1930s, Katharine Hepburn showed just how clever a comedienne she could be alongside Cary Grant in four films. In *The Philadelphia Story*, she plays a woman beyond any moral reproach who is married to a highly unconventional husband, C.K. Dexter Haven (surely one of the best names ever in cinema), who has a fondness for drink. First she throws him out of the house and then she divorces him. On the eve of her second marriage, this time to conventional George Kittredge, she meets her Waterloo when, very much the worse for drink, she goes skinny-dipping with Mike, a journalist wonderfully portrayed by James Stewart, who won an Oscar for best male lead. Her strait-laced fiancé cannot forgive her this moral indiscretion and fails to turn up on their wedding day. With her humiliation in front of the wedding party imminent, Cary Grant saves the day and steps up to the altar with her for a second time.

Like so many other films, *The Philadelphia Story* also underwent a remake called *High Society*. There are film buffs who greatly admire this 1956 movie starring Bing Crosby, Grace Kelly and Frank Sinatra, and for which Cole Porter composed a number of songs that almost turned it into a musical. Appearances by Frank Sinatra and Louis Armstrong and his Band are among the highlights of this remake, although Bing Crosby does fall short of Cary Grant's and Katharine Hepburn's graceful refinement.

> # *"Imagine finding you here!"*
> # *"I'm the type of girl you're liable to find anywhere."*

Bijou's response to Lt. Dan Brent

Seven Sinners 1940

DIRECTOR Tay Garnett; written by: John Meehan, Harry Tugend, based on a story by Ladislas Fodor and Laszlo Vadnay; cinematographer: Rudolph Mate; music: Frank Skinner, Charles Previn; editing: Ted J. Kent

WITH Marlene Dietrich (Bijou Blanche), John Wayne (Lt. Dan Brent), Broderick Crawford (Little Ned), Mischa Auer (Sasha), Albert Dekker (Dr. Martin), Billy Gilbert (Tony), Oscar Homolka (Antro), Anna Lee (Dorothy Henderson)

Following Marlene Dietrich's great success in her first comedy *Destry Rides Again*, Universal, her studio, wanted to strike while the iron was still hot and, offering her twice as much again, hired her to star in another comedy. In *Seven Sinners* she plays a second-rate singer called Bijou Blanche who appears in various Pacific island bars, with a drunken ship's doctor, a pickpocket and a devoted sailor called Little Ned in tow (played with notable simple-mindedness by Broderick Crawford). The four of them are deported regularly and go in search of another island.

In the *Seven Sinners* bar on the island of Boni Komba, Bijou finally meets navy lieutenant Dan Brent (John Wayne), who falls hopelessly in love with her and who, for her sake, would give up his navy job. To prevent that, she involves him in a brawl and then disappears with her hangers-on. In one of the most seductive scenes, Dietrich appears wearing a white navy uniform to sing "The Man's in the Navy."

Even before shooting started, Dietrich began a passionate affair with John Wayne that was continued over the course of the films they subsequently made together. Altogether their affair lasted three years despite her relationship with the author Erich Maria Remarque and Wayne's second marriage.

"A Kiss is still a kiss, a sigh is just a sigh... and when two lovers woo, they still say 'I love you.'"

Sam playing it again for Ilsa

Casablanca 1942

DIRECTOR Michael Curtiz; written by: Julius J. and Philip G. Epstein, Howard Koch, based on the stageplay *Everybody Comes to Rick's* by Murray Burnett and Joan Alison; cinematographer: Arthur Edeson; music: Max Steiner; editing: Owen Marks

WITH Humphrey Bogart (Richard ›Rick‹ Blaine), Ingrid Bergman (Ilsa Lund), Paul Henreid (Victor Laszlo), Claude Rains (Captain Renault), Peter Lorre (Ugarte), Conrad Veidt (Major Strasser), Sydney Greenstreet (Senor Ferrari), Curt Bois (pickpocket)

So much has already been written about this cult film and its renowned components: the legendary pair of lovers played by Ingrid Bergman and Humphrey Bogart, the song "As Time Goes By," the venue Rick's Café, Bogart's trenchcoat and the end of the film that sees the beginning of a "wonderful friendship" between Rick and the French Captain Renault.

In terms of its wealth of quotable lines, the film is a match for Shakespeare and illustrates that the most moving love stories are those without a happy ending—although the film-makers were unclear about this for quite some time. Until just before the last days of shooting the film, the director, the script writers and the producer disagreed on who Ilsa Lund should get in the end. The script was changed repeatedly and the actors had to learn their lines anew each day. But finally Ilsa Lund (Ingrid Bergman), who cannot decide between her love for Rick and her duty to her husband Victor Laszlo (Paul Henreid) is persuaded by Rick that she belongs at her husband's side. Shakespeare himself could not have done it better.

Casablanca won three Oscars including one for Michael Curtiz's direction. How would the film have turned out if the director had stuck to the lead roles as first proposed, Ronald Reagan and Ann Sheridan?

Humphrey Bogart and
Ingrid Bergman in private

"Lawyers should never marry other lawyers."

Kip Lurie's advice to the Bonners, claiming that such inbreeding only leads to "idiot children and more lawyers"

Adam's Rib 1949

DIRECTOR George Cukor; written by: Ruth Gordon, Garson Kanin; cinematographer: George J. Folsey; music: Miklos Rozsa; editing: George Boemler

WITH Katharine Hepburn (Amanda Bonner), Spencer Tracy (Adam Bonner), Judy Holliday (Doris Attinger), Tom Ewell (Warren Attinger), David Wayne (Kip Lurie), Jean Hagen (Beryl Caighn), Hope Emerson (Olympia La Pere), Eve March (Grace)

Spencer Tracy and Katharine Hepburn in another of their films, *Woman of the Year*, 1942

Movie-goers loved the pairing of Katharine Hepburn and Spencer Tracy. Long gone were the days when studio bosses viewed the actress as bad news at the box office. One film after another followed in quick succession with them both in the leading roles. It was known that in private, too, they were a couple. Hollywood knew and, in an unusual instance of liberalism, accepted the fact that Tracy was still married and that, as an orthodox Catholic, he would not divorce his wife.

Hepburn and Tracy's sixth film was constructed around a script written by two of their friends, husband and wife Garson Kanin and Ruth Gordon, who would later delight audiences as Maude in the cult film *Harold and Maude*. The essence of the story is based on a real event in which a couple, both lawyers, represented another couple in a court case; he was the prosecution, she the defence for the wife. Thus in court we have not only the case in question, but also the roles of husband and wife under examination. The case unexpectedly turns into a battle of the sexes in which the married lawyers attempt to outdo each other using sharp-tongued and trenchant phrases in dialogues that are brilliantly crafted and for which the two scriptwriters were deservedly nominated for an Oscar.

The minor roles in *Adam's Rib* were filled using New York stage actors who were unknown in Hollywood and whose film careers were launched by the film. Judy Holliday played the accused wife and even won an Oscar for her next role, while Tom Ewell, playing her husband, came to prominence alongside Marilyn Monroe in *The Seven Year Itch*.

"Mademoiselle, there is no happier man in Paris than Monsieur Mulligan at this moment."

Jerry Mulligan after Lise Bouvier finally agrees to keep a date with him

An American in Paris 1951

DIRECTOR Vincente Minnelli; written by: Alan Jay Lerner; cinematography: Alfred Gilks, John Alton; music: George Gershwin; editing: Adrienne Fazan

WITH Leslie Caron (Lise Bouvier), Gene Kelly (Jerry Mulligan), Oscar Levant (Adam Cook), Georges Guétary (Henri Baurel), Nina Foch (Milo Roberts), Eugene Borden (George Mattieu), Martha Bamattre (Mathilde Mattieu), Mary Jones (dancer), Ann Codee (Therese), George Davis (François)

An American in Paris is by far the loveliest Hollywood musical of the 1950s. It took its lead from the music of George Gershwin whose tone poem lent both its name and its tempo to this wonderfully jaunty film.

Gene Kelly, after Fred Astaire the second great male dancer, plays an American painter who, like so many artists, tries his luck in Paris where he meets and falls in love with a petite lady selling perfume for a living, played by a young and whimsical Leslie Caron. Their love story is driven by marvelous dance numbers that were partly choreographed by Gene Kelly himself. Inspired by the paintings and drawings of French artists like Toulouse-Lautrec, Kelly and Caron sail through an enchanted Paris in ever-changing roles and costumes. Seldom has a couple been so well suited to each other. The film won six Oscars, including Best Film of 1951, and Gene Kelly received a special Oscar in recognition of his achievements in choreography in film.

"...it was a wonderful time..."

Jerry Lewis describing the Hollywood years when he and
Dean Martin made two films a year

Sailor Beware 1951

DIRECTOR Hal Walker; written by: James
Allardice, Martin Rackin, based on a play
by Kenyon Nicholson; cinematographer:
Daniel Fapp; music: Joseph J. Lilley; editing: Warren Low

WITH Dean Martin (Al Crowthers), Jerry
Lewis (Melvin Jones), Corinne Calvet
(guest star), Marion Marshall (Hilda Jones),
Robert Strauss (Lardoski), Leif Erickson
(Captain Lane), Don Wilson (Mr. Chubby),
Vince Edwards (Blayden)

A tried and tested team over many years:
Dean Martin (left) and Jerry Lewis in
Jumping Jacks, 1952

One of the most unusual pairs in the film business was Dean Martin
and Jerry Lewis. The "crooner" and the comedian made their official
debut as a duo on July 25, 1946 and worked together for exactly ten
years. At first they took their comedy program into various clubs, large
and small, and over time, they enjoyed greater success with it. In the
end, they were offered $75,000 a night. Jerry Lewis wrote the gags,
played the fool and permanently created a fuss while Dean Martin tried
to sing his songs.

They made their first film together in 1949, the first of sixteen over
a period of seven years. *Sailor Beware* was their sixth. Under a banner of
"sex and slapstick," one that applied equally to their stage shows, Jerry
Lewis as Melvin Jones and Dean Martin as Al Crowthers play two navy
recruits escaping the ladies. At his physical inspection and later in the
navy itself, Jerry Lewis turns everything upside down and is mistaken
for a lady-killer while his great buddy Dean Martin stands by him and
always knows how to prevent the worst from happening. Like the others, this slapstick movie was a great success with the public and took
$72 million at the box office. Both actors were highly successful in their
long-standing partnership and liked to be compared to the legendary
pair of comics, Oliver Hardy and Stan Laurel, but went their own ways
in 1956 following a disagreement and never collaborated again.

"I shouldn't really fall head over heels in love with you…"

Cynthia to Harry

The Snows of Kilimanjaro 1952

DIRECTOR Henry King; written by: Casey Robinson, based on the short story of the same name by Ernest Hemingway; cinematographer: Leon Shamroy; music: Bernard Herrmann; editing: Barbara McLean

WITH Ava Gardner (Cynthia), Gregory Peck (Harry), Susan Hayward (Helen), Hildegarde Neff (Countess Liz), Leo G. Carroll (Uncle Bill), Torin Thatcher (Johnson), Ava Norring (Beatrice), Helene Stanley (Connie), Marcel Dalio (Emile)

Many critics believe *The Snows of Kilimanjaro* to be Gregory Peck's best film. Based on a story by Ernest Hemingway, the film was directed by Henry King, who five years later would also direct the filming of Hemingway's novel *The Sun Also Rises*.

While on a big-game hunt in Africa, author Harry (Gregory Peck) injures himself and thinks he will die from his infected wound. Flashbacks familiarize the audience with Harry's life: his decision not to lead a middle-class life and to become an author instead; his political activism that causes him to join the Republicans in the Spanish Civil War; his first great love that he looses in that war; his Bohemian way of life as an author and his numerous affairs. The woman Peck cannot get out of his mind is Ava Gardner, an actress of decidedly sensuous charm who became the epitome of the seductively feminine and a screen idol during the 1950s in films like *The Barefoot Contessa* and *The Sun Also Rises*. In *The Snows of Kilimanjaro*, Gardner plays Cynthia, the great love of the hero's life. The second woman at Gregory Peck's side was Susan Hayward who took on the role of the devoted wife who cares for her husband, saves his life and helps him to find himself again.

"Remember, honey, on your wedding day it's alright to say 'yes.'"

Dorothy's advice to Loreli on her way to the altar

Gentlemen Prefer Blondes 1953

DIRECTOR Howard Hawks; written by: Charles Lederer, based on a play by Anita Loos and Joseph Fields; cinematographer: Harry J. Wild; music: Lionel Newman; editing: Hugh S. Fowler

WITH Marilyn Monroe (Loreli), Jane Russell (Dorothy), Charles Coburn (Sir Francis Beekman), Elliot Reid (Malone), Tommy Noonan (Gus Esmond), George "Foghorn" Winslow (Henry Spofford III), Marcel Dalio (Magistrate), Taylor Holmes (Gus Esmond Sr.)

Finally there: Jane Russell as Dorothy (left) and Marilyn Monroe as Loreli

This tale of two "Girls from Little Rock" was based on a novel by Anita Loos. Howard Hawks directed the film in which two pretty young things—blond Marilyn Monroe and brunette Jane Russell—set out in search of rich husbands. This was Hawks' second comedy with Marilyn Monroe; the year before, in 1952, they had shot *Monkey Business*. In *Gentlemen Prefer Blondes*, Russell and Monroe shared the leading roles. Both had gone to the same High School and, despite their contrary expectations, became the best of friends during shooting.

Loreli Lee (Monroe) and Dorothy (Russell) lead miserable, precarious lives as singers and dancers. Meeting rich gentlemen on a crossing from New York to France is seen as the answer. Even if marriage does not work out in the long term, the diamonds acquired by the girls would make their future a bit more secure. In the end, both girls find themselves standing in front of the altar, the dreams they had as "Girls from Little Rock" fulfilled.

This lightweight tale delights audiences with wonderful scenes in which the two former pin-up girls Marilyn Monroe and Jane Russell demonstrate their talents as singers and dancers. The scene in which Marilyn sings "Diamonds are a Girl's Best Friend" is among the best to be found in cinematic history. It inspired Madonna's song "Material Girl" and the accompanying video was unashamedly modelled on the film.

"Some countries have a medal for everything."

Elsie's comment to the Grand Duke

The Prince and the Showgirl 1957

DIRECTOR Laurence Olivier; written by: Terence Rattigan, based on his play *The Sleeping Prince*; cinematographer: Jack Cardiff; music: Richard Addinsell, Muir Mathieson; editing: Jack Harris

WITH Marilyn Monroe (Elsie Marina), Laurence Olivier (Grand Duke Charles), Sybil Thorndike (Queen Dowager), Richard Wattis (Northbrooke), Jeremy Spenser (King Nicholas), Esmond Knight (Hoffman), Paul Hardwick (Maître d'hôtel), Rosamund Greenwood (Maud), Aubrey Dexter (ambassador)

When Marilyn Monroe met the famed stage and motion-picture actor Laurence Olivier in 1950 during a reception in his honor, she very much hoped that she would be able to work alongside him one day. The chance arose seven years later when Olivier directed a film version of the romantic play *The Sleeping Prince* in which he and his wife Vivien Leigh had appeared on stage four years earlier. Both for commercial and artistic reasons, it was decided to cast Marilyn Monroe in the role of the Brooklyn showgirl. Accompanied by her new husband Arthur Miller, she travelled to England to shoot the film. The next few months were to prove difficult for everyone involved. Vivien Leigh was jealous of Marilyn who was keen to demonstrate the breadth of her acting skills to the great Olivier—instead, however she was a bag of nerves on set.

A light comedy eventually emerged in which Marilyn played a naïve loving wife who is unable to handle the conventions of the court and who in the end has to relinquish her husband. Laurence Olivier played the part of the dignified ruler.

"Mr. Allen, ... there are some men who don't end every sentence with a proposition."

Jan trying to keep Brad at arm's length

Pillow Talk 1959

DIRECTOR Michael Gordon; written by: Stanley Shapiro, Maurice Richlin, based on a story by Russell Rouse and Clarence Greene; cinematographer: Arthur E. Arling; music: Frank DeVol, Joseph Gershenson; editing: Milton Carruth

WITH Doris Day (Jan Morrow), Rock Hudson (Brad Allen), Tony Randall (Jonathan Forbes), Thelma Ritter (Alma), Nick Adams (Tony Walters), Julia Meade (Marie), Allen Jenkins (Harry), Marcel Dalio (Pierot)

Doris Day, née Doris von Kappelhoff, was for many years a star of the movie musical before a string of comedies made her one of the leading Hollywood actresses of the 1950s and '60s. Her role was that of the down-to-earth and thoroughly decent woman who would not let herself be led astray until she had married her man. In the late 1960s, this gained her the reputation of being squeaky-clean. What was overlooked was that she always played independent and professionally successful women who did not depend on a man to look after them.

In *Pillow Talk*, she plays a busy interior designer who, because of congestion in New York's telephone network, has to share a line with a songwriter who is cheerily played by Rock Hudson. He has made it his habit to delight his numerous lady friends over the phone with his compositions at all times of the day and night. Her attempts to force him to stick to certain times fail regularly so. In an attempt to restore harmony between them, he allows her to re-design his apartment, an opportunity she uses to exact a subtle revenge. In his tastelessly furnished apartment, which includes such useful items as folding beds and doors fitted with automatic locks, the two confront each other. There is, of course, a happy ending to their showdown.

Two years later, these successful comedians made yet another film together, *Lover Come Back*, in which they played two rival advertising agents.

Doris Day and Rock Hudson remained close friends off set. When news broke in 1984 that Rock Hudson was terminally ill with AIDS, she was one of the few people willing to be seen at his side.

"Well, nobody's perfect."

Osgood refuses to take no for an answer

Some Like it Hot 1959

DIRECTOR Billy Wilder; written by: Billy Wilder und I.A.L. Diamond, based on a story by R. Thoeren and M. Logan; cinematographer: Charles Lang Jr.; music: Adolph Deutsch; editing: Arthur Schmidt

WITH Jack Lemmon (Jerry/Daphne), Tony Curtis (Joe/Josephine), Marilyn Monroe (›Sugar Kane‹), George Raft (›Spats‹ Colombo), Pat O'Brien (Mulligan), Joe E. Brown (Osgood E. Fielding III), Nehemiah Persoff (Little Bonaparte)

Joe and Sugar Kane: Tony Curtis and Marilyn Monroe during the filming

Billy Wilder probably ranks alongside Ernst Lubitsch as the best comedy director in the history of cinema. With a light touch, spot-on timing and lots of puns, he presents us with the most entertaining and absurd situations, among them the story of two musicians, Joe (Tony Curtis) and Jerry (Jack Lemmon) who witness a massacre in Chicago on Valentine's Day and who, in the company of an all-female combo, then flee to Florida dressed as women.

Generations of movie-goers have since been delighted by what Curtis and Lemmon make of their roles as female musicians. They are joined by Marilyn Monroe playing Sugar Kane, a woman disappointed in love and with a strong penchant for drink. She is now hoping for a lucky break, preferably in the shape of a millionaire. Tony Curtis fills that role and with his portrayal of the wealthy man incapable of love, he paid homage to an actor greatly admired by him, Cary Grant.

The film introduced audiences to another "perfect couple," however: Osgood Fielding III (Joe E. Brown), a millionaire looking for another wife, and Jerry/Daphne (Jack Lemmon) who so thoroughly convinces himself that he is a woman that he allows Osgood to court him according to all the rules in the book. When Osgood finally asks "her" for "her" hand, "she" can only admit at the last moment: "But I'm a man!" Osgood's disarming comment that "Nobody is perfect" resolves the tricky situation.

"Take my breath away..."

Marc Antony, dying in Cleopatra's arms

Cleopatra 1963

DIRECTOR Joseph L. Mankiewicz; written by: Joseph L. Mankiewicz, Ranald Mac-Dougall, Sidney Buchman, based on texts by Plutarch, Appian and Suetonius, and on the novel *The Life and Times of Cleopatra* by Carlo Mario Franzero; cinematographer: Leon Shamroy; music: Alex North; editing: Dorothy Spencer

WITH Elizabeth Taylor (Cleopatra), Richard Burton (Mark Antony), Rex Harrison (Julius Caesar), Pamela Brown (high priestess), George Cole (Flavius), Hume Cronyn (Sosigenes), Cesare Danova (Apollodorus), Kenneth Haigh (Brutus), Martin Landau (Rufio)

Elizabeth Taylor and Richard Burton during the filming of *Cleopatra*

Shooting of the monumental historical epic that was *Cleopatra* occupies a unique position in movie history because it is among the most scandal-ridden that Hollywood ever saw. Preliminary work on the film started as early as 1958 but it would be another four years before it was finally completed. Shooting, and in particular the grandiose props and costumes, cost vast sums of money and exceeded the original budget of one million dollars many times over. Elizabeth Taylor at first demanded a fee of one million dollars, but had to make do with 750,000 dollars, yet thanks to special clauses in her contract, finally earned almost two million dollars from the film. The first director, Rouben Mamoulian, had to go and his successor, Joseph L. Mankiewicz, could only be freed from another contract with a hefty payment. The script was re-written continuously until the last minute. Elizabeth Taylor fell ill several times and almost died of pneumonia. Agreement was reached at the last minute that Richard Burton would play the role of Mark Antony, although he ended up sitting around in Rome for almost three months before he was needed on set.

All the difficulties surrounding the production were eclipsed, however, by the news that the newly-wed Elizabeth Taylor was having an affair with Richard Burton, who was also married. At a time when such news could still create problems for a film's release, the studio bosses watched developments apprehensively, while hundreds of paparazzi enthusiastically pursued the two lovers. For Elizabeth Taylor and Richard Burton, shooting *Cleopatra* meant the start of a long-term personal and professional relationship that would see them take their civil marriage vows twice and co-star in ten feature films and one television film.

"She's so deliciously low. So horribly dirty."

Professor Higgins' appraisal of Eliza

My Fair Lady 1964

DIRECTOR George Cukor; written by: Alan Jay Lerner, based on a musical by Alan Jay Lerner and Frederick Loewe and on the drama *Pygmalion* by George Bernard Shaw; cinematographer: Harry Stradling; music: Frederick Loewe, Andre Previn; editing: William Ziegler

WITH Audrey Hepburn (Eliza Doolittle), Rex Harrison (Prof. Henry Higgins), Stanley Holloway (Alfred P. Doolittle), Wilfried Hyde-White (Colonel Hugh Pickering), Gladys Cooper (Mrs. Higgins), Jeremy Brett (Freddy Eynsford-Hill), Theodore Bikel (Zoltan Karpathy), Isobel Elsom (Mrs. Eynsford-Hill), John McLiam (Harry)

My Fair Lady was first a huge hit as a Broadway musical, then a cinema box-office success. The run for the leading female role was between the beautiful Audrey Hepburn and the Broadway star Julie Andrews. Hepburn won and was cast as Eliza Doolittle, the common flower-seller transformed into a high-society lady by linguist Professor Henry Higgins, played by Rex Harrison in one of his best roles. He so perfectly portrayed the pedantic academic in his varying moods that Hollywood had no choice but to present him with an Oscar.

Cary Grant had been offered the role of eccentric Henry Higgins, but did not in the end get it because of his petty objections to the script. He was somewhat aggrieved afterwards.

The film's exceptional costumes were the work of Cecil Beaton and still make an impression today. Madonna drew on them, in fact, for inspiration for her *Justify My Love* world tour.

"Wouldn't it have been lovely if we'd met before?"

Lara to Yuri

Doctor Zhivago 1965

DIRECTOR David Lean; written by: Robert Bolt, based on the novel of the same name by Boris Pasternak; cinematographer: Freddie Young; music: Maurice Jarre; editing: Norman Savage

WITH Julie Christie (Lara), Geraldine Chaplin (Tonya), Omar Sharif (Yuri), Rod Steiger (Komarovsky), Alec Guinness (Yevgraf), Tom Courtenay (Pasha/Strelnikoff), Siobhan McKenna (Anna)

Geraldine Chaplin as Tonya with Omar Sharif

Great film epics would appear to need literary models. The successful director David Lean (*The Bridge on the River Kwai, Lawrence of Arabia*) chose to film Nobel prize winner Boris Pasternak's best-selling novel and turned it into a film of more than three hours' duration. Even the opening credits accompanied by Maurice Jarre's theme tune of "Lara's Theme" captivated audiences.

Using a host of first-rate actors, including Omar Sharif, Julie Christie, Geraldine Chaplin, Rod Steiger, Alec Guinness and Tom Courtenay, the film tells the story of doctor and lyric poet Uri Zhivago, played by Sharif. Set against the backdrop of Russian history from tsarist to Stalinist rule, the film paints a picture of an era by illustrating the fates of a number of individuals. Throughout his life, Zhivago is torn between his wife Tonya (Geraldine Chaplin) and his inspiration and lover Lara (played by the lovely Julie Christie). Political events cause the three of them to be parted and re-united frequently.

The film is driven by the intense interaction between all the protagonists and superb landscapes that were actually shot in Finland because the Soviet Union was out of bounds as a location. *Doctor Zhivago* was nominated for the Best Film Oscar, but lost out to *The Sound of Music*, a decision that even at the time did not please the critics.

"This here's Miss Bonnie Parker. I'm Clyde Barrow. We rob banks."

Clyde Barrow

Bonnie and Clyde 1967

DIRECTOR Arthur Penn; written by: David Newman, Robert Benton; cinematographer: Burnett Guffey; music: Charles Strouse; editing: Dede Allen

WITH Warren Beatty (Clyde Barrow), Faye Dunaway (Bonnie Parker), Gene Hackman (Buck Barrow), Estelle Parsons (Blanche), Michael J. Pollard (C.W. Moss), Denver Pyle (Frank Hamer), Gene Wilder (Eugene Grizzard)

Set during the Great Depression of the 1930s, *Bonnie & Clyde* is the tale of a pair of itinerant bank robbers who, finally cornered by the police, perish in a hail of bullets. Nominated for a Best Film Oscar, the film also made an Oscar-nominated star of the previously unknown Faye Dunaway whose beret became a piece of fashion history.

Until final decisions were taken, the scriptwriters had other options in mind. Originally they had pencilled in Frenchmen Truffaut and Godard as directors. Next under discussion was Warren Beatty who was interested both in directing and producing the film. His sister, Shirley McLaine, was to have played Bonnie. In the end, Beatty was chosen as male lead, Arthur Penn was to direct the film and, after two film productions, a relatively unknown Faye Dunaway was hired to play the part of Bonnie. Beatty and Dunaway became lovers for a short time. Beatty was known as a womanizer fond of an affair with his leading lady.

The film was a success not only artistically, but financially too. Penn was accused, however, of showing scenes of gratuitous violence. He countered his critics by saying that violent scenes were part and parcel of a realistic portrayal of life.

"Are we getting married tomorrow?"– "No…"–"Day after tomorrow?"

Ben trying to make up Elaine's mind

The Graduate 1967

DIRECTOR Mike Nichols; written by: Calder Willingham, Buck Henry, based on the novel of the same name by Charles Webb; cinematographer: Robert Surtees; music: Dave Grusin; editing: Sam O'Steen

WITH Anne Bancroft (Mrs. Robinson), Katharine Ross (Elaine Robinson), Dustin Hoffman (Ben Braddock), William Daniels (Mr. Braddock), Murray Hamilton (Mr. Robinson), Elizabeth Wilson (Mrs. Braddock), Brian Avery (Carl Smith), Walter Brooke (Mr. Maguire), Elisabeth Fraser (lady)

Mrs. Robinson's leg – Ben cannot say "no"

The Graduate launched the career of a young actor who has since shown himself to be one of the most versatile performers of his generation: Dustin Hoffman. The role of the inexperienced graduate Benjamin Braddock, who is seduced by the wife of one of his father's business partners, suited him to a tee. In the original novel, Ben was a blond surfer, but when director Mike Nichols attended screen tests with Katharine Ross, who was to play the role of the daughter Elaine, he knew that the insecure and shy Dustin Hoffmann would do the role justice. Besides Katharine Ross as Elaine, Anne Bancroft as Mrs. Robinson also gave a highly convincing performance as the married woman bored with her husband and who wants to spice up her life by starting an affair with Ben, but who finds it unbearable that he sincerely falls in love with her daughter.

The film was an out-and-out hit, taking $30 million within seven months and had the critics heaping praise on it, although conservative voices found fault with its tale of adultery. *The Graduate* received five awards: Golden Globes were presented to Anne Bancroft, Katharine Ross, Dustin Hoffmann and the director Mike Nichols. All four of them were later nominated for an Oscar, but with competition that year strong, only Mike Nichols succeeded in winning the award.

"You can't spend the rest of your life crying. It annoys people in the movies."

Oscar complaining to Felix

The Odd Couple 1968

DIRECTOR Gene Saks; written by: Neil Simon, based on his play; cinematographer: Robert B. Hauser; music: Neal Hefti; editing: Frank Bracht

WITH Jack Lemmon (Felix Ungar), Walter Matthau (Oscar Madison), John Fiedler (Vinnie), Herb Edelman (Murray), David Sheiner (Roy), Larry Haines (Speed), Monica Evans (Cecily), Carole Shelley (Gwendolyn)

Billy Wilder was the first to recognize the potential of Walter Matthau and Jack Lemmon as acting partners. He cast them alongside each other in his 1966 film *The Fortune Cookie* in which Jack Lemmon played a television reporter who, at the bidding of his unscrupulous brother-in-law—played by Walter Matthau—feigns a serious injury in an attempt to defraud his health insurance scheme.

Two years later, Gene Saks engaged Matthau and Lemmon to tell the stories of two entirely different men. Oscar Madison, played by Walter Matthau, is a sports reporter and disorder personified. His home meets his most basic needs and is first and foremost the venue for poker games with his buddies. Empty beer cans and ashtrays brimming with cigarette ends are proof of their numerous games, and add to the ambience.

One of his friends, the pernickety and compulsively clean Felix Ungar—played by a uniquely accomplished Jack Lemmon—is thrown out of his house but he finds refuge at Oscar's. The battle is now joined between good and evil, between cleanliness and dirtiness, between appetizing snacks with beer in glasses and french fries with beer straight from the can....

This was a spectacularly good film. And it was obvious just how much scope for development it had. From it arose the television series called *The Odd Couple* in which Tony Randall and Jack Klugman took on the star roles.

Friends Jack Lemmon and Walter Matthau went on to make many films together, including the 1998 continuation of their story as an odd couple.

"If he'd just pay me what he's paying them to stop me robbing him, I'd stop robbing him!"

Butch's new business plan

Butch Cassidy and the Sundance Kid 1969

DIRECTOR George Roy Hill; written by: William Goldman; cinematographer: Conrad Hall; music: Burt Bacharach; editing: John C. Howard, Richard C. Meyer

WITH Paul Newman (Butch Cassidy), Robert Redford (Sundance Kid), Katharine Ross (Etta Place), Strother Martin (Percy Garris), Henry Jones (bicycle salesman), Jeff Corey (Sheriff Bledsoe), George Furth (Woodcock), Ted Cassidy (Harvey Logan)

The great era of the Western was already in decline when an unusual film gave the genre a new boost. It was based on the true story of the outlaws Butch Cassidy and Sundance Kid, who in the 1880s and '90s were highly successful bank and train robbers. To save themselves from their pursuers, they had to flee to Bolivia where they were eventually ambushed and killed.

Author William Goldman created a superb film script out of the material. When it came to casting, it was agreed that Paul Newman should play Sundance Kid; those considered for the role of Butch Cassidy ranged from Warren Beatty and Steve McQueen to Marlon Brando. None of the decision makers wanted Robert Redford for the role as he had made a good impression only once before, in a film called *Barefoot in the Park*. But director George Roy Hill trusted his intuition and insisted on hiring Redford. The studio bosses finally relented and both actors reached an agreement that resulted in Newman playing Butch Cassidy and Redford taking the role of Sundance Kid.

Gripping from start to finish, *Butch Cassidy and the Sundance Kid* proved to be the most successful Western ever at the box office and was nominated for the Best Film Oscar that year. A sequel telling the story of Etta Place and starring Katharine Ross, Sundance Kid's mistress, but did not match the success of its predecessor. Newman and Redford, however, later also starred alongside each other in another successful film: *The Sting* (1973).

"Love means never having to say you're sorry."

Oliver Barrett IV

Love Story 1970

DIRECTOR Arthur Hiller; written by: Erich Segal, based on his novel; cinematographer: Dick Kratina; music: Francis Lai; editing: Robert C. Jones

WITH Ali MacGraw (Jennifer Cavilleri), Ryan O'Neal (Oliver Barrett IV), Ray Milland (Oliver Barrett III), Katharine Balfour (Mrs. Oliver Barrett III), John Marley (Phil Cavilleri), Russell Nype (Dean Thompson), Sydney Walker (Dr. Shapely), Tommy Lee Jones (Hank)

This love story involving the then little-known actors Ryan O'Neal and Ali MacGraw was by far the most successful film of 1971. It was based on the eponymous best-selling novel by Yale professor Erich Segal. In the midst of the period's difficult avant-garde films, this tragic, but sentimental film proved to be something special, and everybody saw it.

The story is not a new one: handsome and successful Harvard student Oliver Barrett IV, the scion of an old and wealthy Boston family—played by Ryan O'Neal—falls in love with the poor Italian-American Jennifer Cavilleri—Ali MacGraw in her second major role—who is a scholarship student at Radcliffe College. Oliver's parents are opposed to the liaison, but the two marry nonetheless. When Oliver's father stops paying his son's living expenses, he and Jennifer get by on odd jobs. When all hardship appears to have been overcome—Oliver begins practicing as a lawyer, he and Jennifer move into a smart apartment and their thoughts turn to starting a family—Jennifer learns that she is terminally ill with leukaemia. Any dreams of a happy ending are now forgotten. The hospital scene where Oliver crawls into bed to lie beside his dying wife is utterly compelling and had audiences in floods of tears.

Love Story was nominated for seven Oscars, but won only one for a score by Francis Lai that perfectly captured the mood of the film.

The success of *Love Story* resulted in immediate offers of work for both leads. Ryan O'Neal was hired for *What's Up, Doc?* with Barbra Streisand, and Steve McQueen wanted Ali MacGraw as the leading lady in his film *The Getaway*. Come the end of shooting, they were a couple.

"Vice, virtue, it's best not to be too moral — you cheat yourself out of too much life. Aim above morality."

Maude's advice to Harold

Harold and Maude 1971

DIRECTOR Hal Ashby; written by: Colin Higgins; cinematographer: John A. Alonzo; music: Cat Stevens; editing: William A. Sawyer, Edward Warschilka

WITH Ruth Gordon (Maude), Bud Cort (Harold), Vivian Pickles (Mrs. Chasen), Cyril Cusack (sculptor), Charles Tyner (Uncle Victor), Ellen Geer (Sunshine), Eric Christmas (priest), Judy Engles (Candy Gulf)

This story of a love affair between a twenty-year-old young man and a woman almost four times his age was one of the most unusual films of 1971. The critics disliked it, but younger audiences were smitten and turned it into a cult film.

A black comedy, the film tells the tale of Harold, a young man apparently weary of life who delights in attending strangers' funerals and who scuppers his mother's attempts to get him to marry by making ever more imaginative attempts on his life. At one of his 'own' funerals, he meets an old lady called Maude. The audience suspects that there is more to her, more than what they are told: she was imprisoned in a concentration camp where she lost her husband. The old lady lives life to the full, ignores all the social conventions and is not averse to stealing the odd car or a police motorbike on which she tears around the place with her new friend and lover, Harold, as her pillion. When he eventually wants her to marry him, she commits suicide, but not without first telling him that she hopes he will lead a happy life.

Having written highly successful film scripts with her husband, Garson Kanin, in the 1940s and '50s, Ruth Gordon gave one of her best performances as Maude and, advanced in years, still came to enjoy fame and honor as an actress. For her portrayal of the enigmatic neighbor in *Rosemary's Baby*, she won the Oscar for Best Supporting Actress in 1968.

"Rich women never marry poor men…"

Daisy explains to Gatsby why she had refused to marry him

The Great Gatsby 1974

DIRECTOR Jack Clayton; written by: Francis Ford Coppola, based on the novel of the same name by F. Scott Fitzgerald; cinematographer: Douglas Slocombe; music: Nelson Riddle; editing: Tom Priestley

WITH Mia Farrow (Daisy Buchanan), Robert Redford (Jay Gatsby), Bruce Dern (Tom Buchanan), Karen Black (Myrtle Wilson), Scott Wilson (George Wilson), Sam Waterston (Nick Carraway), Lois Chiles (Jordan Baker), Howard da Silva (Meyer Wolfsheim), John Devlin (bodyguard)

The craze for nostalgia that made its mark on fashion and the visual arts in the early 1970s did not stop at film. Thus the idea was born to make another film version of F. Scott Fitzgerald's cult novel *The Great Gatsby*, already filmed twice, but without much success. Ali MacGraw had long been earnmarked for the female lead before the decision was taken to hire the sublime Mia Farrow. There were a number of actors interested in the male lead, including Warren Beatty and Jack Nicholson, but in the end the role was given to Robert Redford, who was determined to play Gatsby. Redford was by then a superstar with a string of hugely successful movies under his belt, and he had just given a brilliant performance, along with Paul Newman, in *The Sting*, a film that landed seven Oscars.

The Great Gatsby became a spectacular period picture that aimed to rekindle the spirit of the 1920s down to the last detail. The suits, for instance, were by Ralph Lauren, who was then still an exclusive sports outfitter and not yet an internationally known fashion designer. The film revelled in captivating images of the tragic lovers Gatsby and Daisy, and was trailed massively before its launch. Even that was not enough to prevent it from being thought long-drawn-out, however, and it was a box-office failure.

"Well, tell me, why did you get a divorce?"

Ike to Mary

Manhattan 1978

DIRECTOR Woody Allen; written by: Woody Allen, Marshall Brickman; cinematographer: Gordon Willis; music: George Gershwin; editing: Susan E. Morse

WITH Woody Allen (Isaac Davis, known as ›Ike‹, for short), Diane Keaton (Mary Wilke), Michael Murphy (Yale), Mariel Hemingway (Tracy), Meryl Streep (Jill), Anne Byrne (Emily), Karen Ludwig (Connie), Michael O'Donoghue (Dennis)

The man who created the loveliest films about New York and its inhabitants is undoubtedly Woody Allen, and the loveliest of all his productions is his black-and-white *Manhattan* whose very beginning pays homage to the city. Playing Isaac Davis himself, he declares, "Chapter one. He worshipped New York." And while the author tries to find the right words to describe his enthusiasm *and* with which to open his first novel, the director presents us with a wonderful sequence of a host of images of Manhattan accompanied by George Gershwin's "Rhapsody in Blue."

Here begins the tale of the neurotic Isaac and the two women in his life—seventeen-year-old Tracy, played by Mariel Hemingway, the great author's niece, and the equally neurotic Mary Wilke, played by Allen's long-time partner Diane Keaton. A man who must decide between his job as a television scriptwriter and a freelance author, Isaac must live a life that cannot be really good but that is still too short.

Woody Allen collaborates with the same people again and again. The credits in his films remain unchanged for years at a time, and he likes to give his current wife or partner the female lead in his films—if she happens to be an actress. With two broken marriages behind him, he moved in with Diane Keaton in 1972. They would go on to make six films together, including the successful *Annie Hall,* for which they each won an Oscar, he for directing it, and she as the best female lead. *Manhattan* was their last collaboration. They split and a short while later, Mia Farrow appeared both at Allen's side and in his films.

"We're on a mission from God!"

Elwood's answer to everything

The Blues Brothers 1980

DIRECTOR John Landis; written by: John
Landis, Dan Aykroyd; cinematographer:
Stephen M. Katz; music: Ira Newborn;
editing: George Folsey Jr.

WITH John Belushi (Jake Blues), Dan
Aykroyd (Elwood Blues), James Brown
(Father Cleophus James), Kathleen Free-
man (Sister Mary Stigmata), Cab Calloway
(Curtis), Ray Charles (Ray), Aretha
Franklin (café owner), John Lee Hooker
(Street Slim), Henry Gibson (Nazi), John
Candy (Burton Mercer), Steve Cropper
(Steve 'The Colonel' Cropper), Tom Malone
('Bones' Malone), Lou Marini ('Blue' Lou
Marini), Matt Murphy (Matt 'Guitar'
Murphy)

Based on the totally mad screenplay that Dan Aykroyd co-wrote with
director John Landis, *The Blues Brothers* introduces us to the crankiest
"perfect couple" of them all: John Belushi and Dan Aykroyd.

Aykroyd plays Elwood Blues who goes to collect his brother Jake
(John Belushi) on his release from jail after three years behind bars.
They thunder off home in their "Bluesmobile" only to be told that their
orphanage needs 5,000 dollars to pay a tax bill. To help the orphanage
director, Sister Mary, they hit on the idea of resurrecting their old band
and, "in the name of the Lord," they set off in search of their old buddies in what turns out to be one hell of a trip. They cross the path of a
country and western outfit and pick a fight with a group of neo-Nazis,
are besieged by men in every uniform the United States has to offer
and end up being chased by 150 police cars. This crazy film even offers
a startling succession of musical highlights: musicians such as Cab
Calloway, Ray Charles, James Brown, John Lee Hooker, Aretha Franklin
and many others agreed to appear in it.

A lunatic tale, this film is a pleasure from beginning to end and
immediately achieved cult status.

Dan Aykroyd (left, in both photos) and
John Belushi as the Blues Brothers

"You really don't know me."

John to Elizabeth

Nine ½ Weeks   1986

DIRECTOR Adrian Lyne; written by: Patricia Knop, Zalman King, Sarah Kernochan, based on a novel by Elizabeth McNeill; cinematographer: Peter Biziou; music: Jack Nitzsche, Michael Hoenig; editing: Tom Rolf, Caroline Biggerstaff, Mark Winitsky, Kim Secrist

WITH Kim Basinger (Elizabeth), Mickey Rourke (John), Margaret Whitton (Molly), David Margulies (Harvey), Christine Baranski (Thea), Karen Young (Sue), William De Acutis (Ted), Dwight Weist (Farnsworth), Roderick Cook (Sinclair)

Adrian Lyne's *Nine ½ Weeks* is an erotic thriller in a class of its own. Starting like a romantic love story, it tells the tale of Elizabeth (Kim Basinger), a gallery owner who, with a girlfriend, goes out shopping and sees a guy she immediately fancies. Seemingly by chance, she again meets John (Mickey Rourke), a stockbroker, the next day and he begins to court her in a very unusual way. She embarks on an affair that will last 9 ½ weeks, one that will take her experiences to new limits. John's pleasure comes from having her submit totally to his unconventional and peculiar sexual desires. She is attracted by his enigmatic reserve and goes along with his game of lust and humiliation that sees her becoming increasingly sexually dependent on him. She manages to save herself at the very last moment before reaching the point of no return. After his drastic abuse of her and her trust in him, he remains cold and has no inkling of what he has destroyed.

Adrian Lyne had previously worked as a film-maker in advertising and knew how to present Kim Basinger's body to best effect. The former model was at first unwilling to shoot the film, but was persuaded to take on the role by Lyne and Rourke. For her as an actress, too, the film meant a whole host of new experiences and she finally viewed it as a challenge to which she rose admirably. The film was a great success at the box office and achieved cult status.

There are two versions of the film: one for the European market and another, with some sex scenes expurgated, for the American market. Both, however, include Basinger's famous striptease scene to Joe Cocker's equally famous song "You Can Leave Your Hat on."

"Dance with me." – "Here?" – "Here."

Baby visits Johnny in his room

Dirty Dancing 1987

DIRECTOR Emile Ardolino; written by: Eleanor Bergstein; cinematographer: Jeff Jur; music: John Morris; editing: Peter C. Frank

WITH Jennifer Grey (Frances "Baby" Houseman), Patrick Swayze (Johnny Castle), Jerry Orbach (Dr. Jake Houseman), Cynthia Rhodes (Penny Johnson), Jack Weston (Max Kellerman), Jane Brucker (Lisa Houseman), Kelly Bishop (Marjorie Houseman), Lonny Price (Neil Kellerman)

It left the critics cold but Patrick Swayze fans loved it and *Dirty Dancing* took its place in a line of dance films that had box-office tills ringing in the 1980s. Up until then, Patrick Swayze was better known to television viewers through his role in the six-part series *The North and the South*. Here he plays a dancing teacher, Johnny Castle, who in his spare time practices "dirty dances" with his pupils and is determined to win a summer dancing competition. To this end, he flirts with Frances "Baby" Houseman (Jennifer Grey), the pretty daughter of hotel guests, something strictly forbidden to hotel staff. Matters are further complicated for Johnny by a pregnant girlfriend, who he decides to help in her difficulty. All his problems are finally resolved, and the pretty daughter shows her parents *just how* much she has matured during the holidays when she partners Johnny at the dance competition. The film is driven by the dance sequences in which Patrick Swayze shows how talented he is. He proves that he can sing well, too, in the title song "I've Had the Time of My Life" that later became a chart hit.

Because the film was so successful, a television series of the same name was immediately produced in which the main roles were taken by Patrick Cassidy, the brother of pop singer David Cassidy, and Melora Hardin. The thirty-minute series was shown on American television in 1988 and 1989.

"It's beyond my control."

Vicomte de Valmont explaining to Madame de Tourvel
why he must end their relationship

Dangerous Liaisons 1988

DIRECTOR Stephen Frears; written by: Christopher Hampton, based on the epistolary novel *Les liaisons dangereuses* by Choderlos de Laclos; cinematographer: Philippe Rousselot; music: George Fenton; editing: Mick Audsley

WITH Glenn Close (Marquise de Merteuil), John Malkovich (Vicomte de Valmont), Michelle Pfeiffer (Madame de Tourvel), Swoosie Kurtz (Madame de Volanges), Uma Thurman (Cecile de Volanges), Keanu Reeves (Chevalier Danceny), Mildred Natwick (Madame de Rosemonde)

Madame de Tourvel (Michelle Pfeiffer) succumbs to Valmont's seductive charms

Rare as it is for two directors to make use of the same literary model simultaneously and independently of each other, it happened in the spring of 1988. Both Stephen Frears and Milos Forman turned to Christopher Hampton's stage adaptation of the epistolary novel by eighteenth-century Frenchman, Pierre Choderlos de Laclos. Each had definite ideas about the type of film he wanted to produce, but in the event, the young British director Frears' superb version of *Dangerous Liaisons* trumped *Valmont*, the film by doyen Forman.

As his leading lady, Frears chose a top-form Glenn Close to play the scheming and love-starved Marquise de Merteuil. Around Close he gathered a group of young actors who would themselves subsequently become superstars: John Malkovich, Michelle Pfeiffer, Keanu Reeves and Uma Thurman.

The portrayal of the Vicomte de Valmont—who contrary to expectation falls in love and eventually loses himself in his own and others' intrigues and is finally killed in a duel—marked the launch of a film career for sophisticated actor Malkovich that would transform him into a star of numerous screen adaptations, including *The Sheltering Sky*, *Of Mice and Men*, *Heart of Darkness* and *The Portrait of a Lady*, and which would even see him take the lead role in a film bearing his own name: *Being John Malkovich*.

"You and I are such similar creatures, Vivian. We both screw people for money."

Edward to Vivian

Pretty Woman 1989

DIRECTOR Garry Marshall; written by: J.F. Lawton; cinematographer: Charles Minsky; music: James Newton Howard; editing: Priscilla Nedd

WITH Richard Gere (Edward Lewis), Julia Roberts (Vivian), Ralph Bellamy (James Morse), Laura San Giacomo (Kit De Luca), Hector Elizondo (Hotel manager), Jason Alexander (Philip Stuckey), Alex Hyde-White (David Morse), Amy Yasbeck (Elizabeth Stuckey), Patrick Richwood (Liftboy)

The Cinderella of the '90s was an L.A. hooker called Vivian played by Julia Roberts. She is hired as an escort for a few days by a wealthy and handsome businessman who ends up asking her to marry him. It wasn't only the sight of an impeccably dressed Richard Gere (wearing Armani) that caused women's hearts to flutter.

You'd be hard put *not* to find a woman who would not like to experience the scenes where Vivian, clutching her lover's credit card, goes shopping with him. And many a woman would love to be able to exact the same subtle revenge on the stuck-up shop assistant who turfs Vivian out of her high-class boutique because of her clothes. She later returns to the shop, her arms full of top-name bags.

This pairing of Julia Roberts and Richard Gere was so successful that Hollywood couldn't resist trying it a second time. *Runaway Bride* was unable, however, to match the huge success of *Pretty Woman.*

"And you better get yourself a damn good lawyer!" – "Best your money can buy."

Oliver and Barbara, realizing that they're going to divorce

The War of the Roses

1989

DIRECTOR Danny DeVito; written by: Michael Leeson, based on the novel of the same name by Warren Adler; cinematographer: Stephen H. Burum; music: David Newman; editing: Lynzee Klingman, Nicholas C. Smith

WITH Kathleen Turner (Barbara Rose), Michael Douglas (Oliver Rose), Danny DeVito (Gavin D'Amato), Marianne Sägebrecht (Susan), Sean Astin (Josh, aged 17), Heather Fairfield (Carolyn, aged 17), G. D. Spradlin (Harry Thurmont), Trenton Teigen (Josh, aged 10), Bethany McKinney (Carolyn, aged 10)

The war between Oliver Rose (Michael Douglas) and Barbara Rose (Kathleen Turner) did not result in quite as many victims as the historic War of the Roses between the houses of Lancaster and York, but bodies there were nevertheless.

Actor Danny DeVito directed this black comedy and took the part of the divorce lawyer. His very first film, *Throw Momma from the Train*, had already shown just how much of an all-rounder he was. A friend of the Roses, he leads the audience through the jungle of a matrimonial conflict that is without parallel. The Roses are a married couple with all the visible trappings of personal and professional success: two healthy kids, an imposing home that is tastefully furnished, a number of expensive cars. But a marital row escalates into deadly conjugal warfare that claims as its victims not only pieces of furniture, the pets and the cars, but even the couple themselves. With great relish, DeVito shows us just how much imagination Oliver and Barbara use to hurt each other. He pees into her soup and she wrecks his sports car using her own SUV. When the two of them come crashing to the ground together with the chandelier after almost two hours, the nastiest marital comedy of all time comes to an end.

"...men and women can't be friends because the sex part always gets in the way."

Harry's law

When Harry Met Sally 1989

DIRECTOR Rob Reiner; written by: Nora Ephron; cinematographer: Barry Sonnenfeld; music: Marc Shaiman, Harry Connick Jr.; editing: Robert Leighton

WITH Meg Ryan (Sally Albright), Billy Crystal (Harry Burns), Carrie Fisher (Marie), Bruno Kirby (Jess), Steven Ford (Joe), Lisa Jane Persky (Alice), Michelle Nicastro (Amanda), Gretchen Palmer (stewardess)

If ever a film was an immediate success, it was this one, a marvellous comedy about two people who finally become a couple, but only at the third attempt. Rob Reiner directed this episodic film with a captivating Meg Ryan and a comical Billy Crystal, who discuss whether friendship without sex is possible between men and women. Eventually they fall in love with each other.

Their story starts when they set off on a long drive from university to New York. So sure are they of themselves that Harry and Sally simply can't get through to each other and they are only too pleased to be able to go their separate ways at journey's end. Years later, the protagonists meet again by chance at the airport. Now working and living with a partner, they find their initial dislike of each other turning into attraction, but it is not until their third meeting, when both are single again, that a great friendship develops which culminates in love and marriage.

The film is full of funny and ingenious scenes. The best, and most often cited, is where Sally robs a self-satisfied Harry of his illusion that he can tell whether his lovers' orgasms are real or merely faked. To the great amazement of the other customers in a restaurant, Sally pretends to have an orgasm, which prompts an older female guest to call the waiter and say: "I'll have what she's having!"

When Harry Met Sally is one of those films that you can watch time and again.

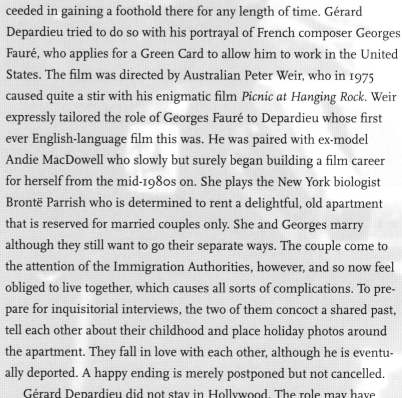

How two strangers got married, met, and then fell in love

Green Card 1990

DIRECTOR Peter Weir; written by: Peter Weir; cinematographer: Geoffrey Simpson; music: Hans Zimmer; editing: William Anderson

WITH Andie MacDowell (Brontë Parrish), Gérard Depardieu (Georges Fauré), Gregg Edelman (Phil), Bebe Neuwirth (Lauren), Robert Prosky (lawyer), Jessie Keosian (Mrs. Bird), Ethan Phillips (Gorsky), Mary Louise Wilson (Mrs. Sheehan), Ronald Guttman (Anton)

Long gone are the days when France exported actors to satisfy Hollywood's demand. In recent years, barely any French stars have succeeded in gaining a foothold there for any length of time. Gérard Depardieu tried to do so with his portrayal of French composer Georges Fauré, who applies for a Green Card to allow him to work in the United States. The film was directed by Australian Peter Weir, who in 1975 caused quite a stir with his enigmatic film *Picnic at Hanging Rock*. Weir expressly tailored the role of Georges Fauré to Depardieu whose first ever English-language film this was. He was paired with ex-model Andie MacDowell who slowly but surely began building a film career for herself from the mid-1980s on. She plays the New York biologist Brontë Parrish who is determined to rent a delightful, old apartment that is reserved for married couples only. She and Georges marry although they still want to go their separate ways. The couple come to the attention of the Immigration Authorities, however, and so now feel obliged to live together, which causes all sorts of complications. To prepare for inquisitorial interviews, the two of them concoct a shared past, tell each other about their childhood and place holiday photos around the apartment. They fall in love with each other, although he is eventually deported. A happy ending is merely postponed but not cancelled.

Gérard Depardieu did not stay in Hollywood. The role may have secured him a Golden Globe as best male actor, but the success he was then enjoying in France—his film *Cyrano de Bergerac* won nine Césars —could not be replicated in the United States.

"Look, you shoot off a guy's head with his pants down..."

Louise telling Thelma why it is not a good idea to drive through Texas
to reach Mexico

Thelma and Louise 1991

DIRECTOR Ridley Scott; written by: Callie Khouri; cinematography: Adrian Biddle, David B. Nowell; music: Hans Zimmer, various songs; editing: Thom Noble

WITH Susan Sarandon (Louise), Geena Davis (Thelma), Harvey Keitel (Hal), Michael Madsen (Jimmy), Christopher McDonald (Darryl), Stephen Tobolowsky (Max), Brad Pitt (J.D.)

The renowned British director Ridley Scott made this first road movie with and for women. Already well known to cinema audiences through his cult science fiction films *Blade Runner* and *Alien*, he directed this tale of two unwilling outlaws with the excellent actresses Susan Sarandon and Geena Davis in the lead roles.

The two friends, waitress Louise Sawyer (Susan Sarandon) and housewife Thelma Dickinson (Geena Davis), really only want to escape their daily routines for a short while and take a trip to the mountains over the weekend. On their first evening in a bar, Thelma chats up the male guests a bit too much for her own good. One of them, who cannot see why a flirt should not lead to more, tries to rape her. Louise shoots the guy and saves Thelma. In panic, the two of them then flee in their car and are soon branded murderesses by the media and are hunted by the police. An understanding cop, warmly played by Harvey Keitel, tries to stop the worst from happening.

Their escape gives them their freedom back again, however. Thelma spends a night making love to a young guy, a fresh-faced Brad Pitt (a conspicuously good piece of casting), who promtly robs her with no compunction.

When they realize that they will be unable to reach the safety of the Mexican border, they choose to die and, in their car, plunge into the Grand Canyon. This tale of two tough women who take their fate into their own hands and accept the consequences of their action was written by a young screenwriter called Callie Khouri, whose work won a Golden Globe and an Oscar for Best Script.

"I would my horse had the speed of your tongue."

Benedick to Beatrice

Much Ado About Nothing 1993

DIRECTOR Kenneth Branagh; written by: Kenneth Branagh, based on the drama of the same name by William Shakespeare; cinematographer: Roger Lanser; music: Patrick Doyle; editing: Andrew Marcus

WITH Emma Thompson (Beatrice), Kenneth Branagh (Benedick), Robert Sean Leonard (Claudio), Keanu Reeves (Don Juan), Denzel Washington (Don Pedro), Michael Keaton (Dogberry), Kate Beckinsale (Hero), Richard Briers (Leonato), Brian Blessed (Antonio), Gerard Horan (Borachio), Richard Clifford (Conrad)

Emma Thompson and Kenneth Branagh with Denzel Washington as Don Pedro

If any director has recently succeeded in adapting Shakespeare's plays for the screen and in turning them into cinematic events, he has Irishman Kenneth Branagh to thank for being able to do so. Branagh gained his first experience acting Shakespeare with the Royal Shakespeare Company, where as Henry V and Hamlet he was acclaimed by critics and audiences alike. He was twenty-eight when he directed *Henry V* off the cuff for the first time. Both as director and leading male, roles he would take on in his later Shakespeare films, his performances immediately convinced everyone.

After tragedy, Branagh turned to comedy. In Tuscany, he brought together a host of young and handsome Hollywood stars like Keanu Reeves, Robert Sean Leonard and Denzel Washington and directed the bard's play about love and trust, envy and foul aspersion. He himself took the role of the confirmed bachelor Benedick who is constantly at loggerheads with Beatrice, a comely maid who is never lost for words, played by his then wife Emma Thompson. It is a real treat to watch how their friends make a match of them. As was customary in Shakespeare's comedies, come the play's end we find at least two couples before the altar—happy even if they haven't quite escaped unscathed.

"Jack, I'm flying..."

Rose on top of the world

Titanic 1997

DIRECTED AND WRITTEN BY James Cameron; cinematographer: Russell Carpenter; music: James Horner; editing: Conrad Buff, James Cameron

WITH Kate Winslet (Rose DeWitt Bukater), Leonardo DiCaprio (Jack Dawson), Billy Zane (Cal Hockley), Kathy Bates (Molly Brown), Bill Paxton (Brock Lovett), Bernard Hill (Captain Smith), Jonathan Hyde (Bruce Ismay), Victor Garber (Thomas Andrews)

The story of the world's most famous shipping disaster in April 1912 had been filmed several times before director James Cameron turned his attention to it. His screen adaptation surpassed everything that had gone before and surprised audiences with new special effects. It went on to become the most successful film ever, taking almost $2 billion at box offices in the United States alone.

The maiden voyage and sinking of the Titanic provide the backdrop for a fictional love story between young and wealthy Rose (Kate Winslet) and artist and third-class passenger Jack Dawson (Leonardo DiCaprio). Kate Winslet had come to prominence especially through her portrayal as Marianne in the screen adaptation of Jane Austen's *Sense and Sensibility*, while Leonardo DiCaprio had impressed audiences as a powerfully expressive and versatile young actor in films like *What's Eating Gilbert Grape* and *Romeo & Juliet*.

In this love story, the two Titanic passengers enjoy their brief happiness unconfined by the barriers of class before the ship collides with an iceberg. Their separation in the water, where Jack perishes and Rose is saved, captured the emotions of many a moviegoer.

Rose and Jack—Kate Winslet and Leonardo DiCaprio—were the Hollywood couple to have attracted the most viewers in the twentieth century.

"It's like seeing someone for the first time, and you look at each other for a few seconds…"

Jack Foley

Out of Sight 1998

DIRECTOR Steven Soderbergh; written by: Scott Frank, based on the novel by Elmore Leonard; cinematographer: Elliot Davis; music: David Holmes; editing: Anne V. Coates

WITH Jennifer Lopez (Karen Sisco), George Clooney (John Michael "Jack" Foley), Ving Rhames (Buddy Bragg), Mike Malone (bank client), Don Cheadle (Maurice "Snoopy" Miller), Dennis Farina (Marshall Sisco)

Take one stunningly handsome actor, one gorgeous actress, one crime thriller as the basis for a screenplay and one good, but not too well-known director, mix them all together and see what the result is. It's an approach that doesn't always work, but in the case of *Out of Sight*, the result was an exciting and sparkling champagne cocktail. Director Steven Soderbergh, whose debut film *Sex, Lies and Videotape* was noticed by a wide audience and who won a Golden Palm in Cannes at his first attempt, is a great fan of crime writer Elmore Leonard on whose books the cult films *Get Shorty* and *Jackie Brown* were also based.

Out of Sight tells the story of experienced bank robber Jack Foley, played by the "sexiest man alive," George Clooney. Jack's success rate —he has held up more than 200 banks with not a gun in sight—still doesn't save him from landing repeatedly in jail from where he escapes with a friend's help until one day Marshall Karen Sisco (singer and actress Jennifer Lopez in a superb piece of casting) crosses his path during another jail-break. Although they become closer while confined in the trunk of the get-away car, she finally manages to escape and spares no effort to see him again and to get him back behind bars.

The air between Jennifer Lopez and George Clooney crackled even at the screen tests, and continued to do so during shooting, lending the film its erotic note.

Jack Foley (George Clooney) with his friend Buddy Bragg (right: Ving Rhames)

Front cover: Ingrid Bergman and Humphrey Bogart
in *Casablanca* (see p. 32)
Back cover: (from top right to bottom right) *The Public
Enemy* (see p. 10), *Ninotchka* (see p. 26), *Tarzan the Ape
Man* (see p. 14), *Adam's Rib* (see p. 34), *The Gay Divorcee*
(see p. 16), *Nine ½ Weeks* (see p. 74)
Main photo and frontispiece: *Some Like it Hot* (see p. 48)

Photographic credits: All material has been provided for
publication by pwe Verlag in Hamburg, with the exception
of the images listed below. The Publisher would like to
thank the staff at defd for their kind cooperation.
p. 50: Deutsches Filminstitut – DIF, Frankfurt
p. 54: Peter W. Engelmeier (ed.), *Film and Fashion*,
Prestel Verlag 1990
pp. 8, 9, 32, 48: Private collection

Die Deutsche Bibliothek CIP-Einheitsaufnahme data and
the Library of Congress Cataloguing-in-Publication data
is available

© Prestel Verlag
Munich · Berlin · London · New York 2002

Prestel Verlag
Mandlstrasse 26, 80802 Munich
Tel. +49 (89) 38 17 09-0
Fax +49 (89) 38 17 09-35

4 Bloomsbury Place, London WC1A 2QA
Tel. +44 (020) 7323-5004
Fax +44 (020) 7636-8004

175 Fifth Avenue, Suite 402,
New York, NY 10010
Tel. +1 (212) 995-2720
Fax +1 (212) 995-2733

www.prestel.com

Concept and picture selection by Gabriele Ebbecke
Translated from the German by Stephen Telfer, Edinburgh
Copyedited by Christopher Wynne

Font: Scala Serif and TheSans
Origination: Repro Ludwig, Zell am See
Printing: Appl, Wemding
Binding: Conzella, Pfarrkirchen

Printed in Germany on acid-free paper

ISBN 3-7913-2691-0